Putting God First: The Tithe

Norma Wimberly

DISCIPLESHIP RESOURCES
MATERIALS FOR GROWTH IN CHRISTIAN FAITH & LIFE
—— NASHVILLE, TENNESSEE ——
P.O. BOX 840 • NASHVILLE, TN 37202 • PHONE (615) 340-7068

Reprinted 1996.

PUTTING GOD FIRST: THE TITHE. Copyright © 1988 by Discipleship Resources. All rights reserved. Printed in the United States of America. No part of this booklet may be reproduced in any manner whatsoever without written permission except in the case of brief quotations embodied in critical articles or reviews. For information address Discipleship Resources Editorial Offices, P. O. Box 840, Nashville, TN 37202.

ISBN 0-88177-058-2

Library of Congress Catalog Card No. 88-71011

DR058

Contents

A Symbol of Response

With the completion of this manual, I began to reflect upon its development and now view the entire process as a miracle. Initially, I could not imagine coordinating a project on tithing. My daily activities included many facets of stewardship education, but disciplined giving made me uncomfortable.

I first began to feel God nudge me toward this project in November 1984. As a new staff person in the Section on Stewardship for a denominational board, I read a book about the tithe. No, my life and pattern of giving did not change then. There was no conversion experience, only a nagging sense of being uncomfortable with my faith and response to God.

For almost two years, there was a struggle, earthly and spiritual, to produce a compilation of scripture passages about giving. Then, I remember the day when I wrote of the possibility of this booklet being produced. That day I openly confronted the nature of my struggle: Sunday after Sunday, payday after payday, I was wrestling with what it is that I have; what I am to do with it; and how I am to offer myself and what I have to God. Was there a symbolic response to God's steadfast and generous love and care?

Slowly, gradually, taking small risks here, larger leaps there, I found a response. Tithing is an action, but it results from a *feeling*. It is a response about which I have a choice. Tithing is a part of spiritual growth in my journey by faith. It is, I have found, not a restriction, but a freedom, a joyous act of worship. It is something I *do* that creates a wellspring of joy, and it is a new beginning. My relationship with and response to God is first in my life.

In May 1985, I met Nan Duerling, a layperson from Maryland, during a stewardship training event for the Baltimore area. We quickly became friends, sharing interests in the church, teaching, and writing. As this booklet began to evolve, I knew I needed help, *lots* of help. I also knew that Nan is a generous giver, a committed tither, *and* a free-lance researcher and writer. She had all the necessary skills to research and summarize the historical traditions and interpretations of tithing in addition to her understanding of God's law and grace. Part 1 is thus her contribution to this manual.

Part 2 is the rich contribution and response of many persons who witness to the effect that the tithe has in their lives.

Part 3 invites you to pursue a fourteen-day personal meditation on tithing.

Part 4 is a group study guide to help you bring your congregation to tithing.

My time of silence about tithing is over. I have struggled with it, avoided it, been uneasy and uncertain. Perhaps you have done that, too. My prayers are with you as you read this booklet. Listen and you will hear them as you move nearer the tithe or as you grow beyond it. May God bless your response.

NORMA W. WIMBERLY

PART 1
Tithing in Our Tradition

Tithing is an ancient principle, dating back to cultures older than Judaism. Although the word *tithe* means a tenth part of something, no one knows exactly how the 10 percent figure was determined. We generally associate tithing with the legal requirements of the Mosaic Law, but the practice began long before the Law was received.

In the Pentateuch, detailed instructions are given about the presentation and use of tithes. Little is said about the tithe in the New Testament, a silence which can be interpreted as an acceptance of the tithe as part of the Law, or an avoidance of the call to tithe when one is saved by grace in Jesus Christ. This history of the Christian church includes periods of emphasis on the tithe, but the reasons for that emphasis differ according to the political or cultural milieu.

Faced with such a variety of teachings and traditions, modern Christians are understandably uncertain about the stance they should take toward tithing. Is it an outmoded, legalistic practice of an agricultural economy? Is it an investment that God will bless and multiply? Or is the tithe to be interpreted and practiced in another way—a way which recognizes God's gracious love and our response to that gift? A survey of the major biblical passages and church traditions related to tithing will enable us to forge a more comprehensive framework within which to explore what the tithe may mean to us as Christian disciples. As you read and reflect on the familiar and the not-so-familiar, open yourself to the possibilities of a new revelation.

The Old Testament Tradition

In Genesis 14:17-24, Abraham is shown offering 10 percent of the spoils of war to Melchizedek, king of Salem and high priest of God. The patriarch's action provides a precedent for paying tithes in Jerusalem.

This point will become more important when the Deuteronomic reforms call for the paying of tithes at the Temple in Jerusalem. Furthermore, Abraham's presentation to one who is the priest validates the giving of tithes to the Levites, a practice which develops hundreds of years later with the establishment of the Mosaic Law. By paying tithes to Melchizedek, who was both king and priest, Abraham inadvertently set the stage for future debates as to whether one's tithe should be paid only to the church or divided between the church and secular organizations, or even the government which cares in an ideal world for many of the persons, such as widows and orphans, who may have been supported by religious tithes to the theocracy.

Another ancestral offering of tithes is recorded in Genesis 28:10-22. Abraham's grandson, Jacob, has a dream in which he sees a vision of God in heaven. Struck by the power of the dream, Jacob acknowledges God and promises to give a tithe "of all thou givest me" if the Lord will care for him on his journey home. This pledge, however, is essentially a *bargain* that Jacob struck with God. Many of us still pray, "God, *if* you will . . . !" We, and our brother, Jacob, struggle for control. We want to manage the results of any response to God!

The tithes of Abraham and Jacob are not presented to fulfill the Law because there *was* no law. When the Law is established, however, prescriptions concerning the collection and use of tithes are set forth in detail. The passage in Leviticus 27:30-33 is an appendix to the Holiness Code in which God proclaims the rules for maintaining a holy relationship with God. The people are expected to give every tenth animal, regardless of its condition, to Yahweh. According to verse 30, "all the tithe of the land . . . is the Lord's; it is holy to the Lord." Since the tithe already belongs to God, persons are only returning what is rightfully God's own.

In Deuteronomy 26:1-11, there is record of a tithe to be given when the wandering Israelites reach Canaan. This tithe of firstfruits is to be given as a sign of thanksgiving for the Lord's deliverance and provision.

Numbers 18:21-32 explains that the tithe is to be given to the Levites. These priests, who serve the Temple, are not eligible to inherit land. God provides for them by commanding the Israelites to pay their tithes to the Levites. The priests, in turn, are required to give the choicest tenth of the tithes they receive as a tithe to the Lord.

According to Deuteronomy 14:22-29, a tenth of seed, grain, wine, oil, and livestock is to be offered annually. This tithe is to be eaten by the tithers at "the place which [the Lord] will choose, to make his name dwell there" (Deut. 14:23). Deuteronomy 12:5-7 and 12:17-19 record that this place is the Temple. If a family lives too far from the Temple to transport their tithe, they are to convert it into cash. When they reach the Temple, they are to use the tithe money to buy whatever they choose. Every three years the household is to give a tithe for charitable purposes to the Levites, widows, and orphans. Whether this tithe is given instead of the one described in 14:22-27, or in addition to it during the third year, is unclear. The Apocryphal book *Tobit,* written a few years before the Christian era, refers to three different tithes, which could amount to as much as 30 percent of one's income in New Testament times.

Often I was quite alone in making the pilgrimage to Jerusalem, fulfilling the Law that binds all Israel perpetually. I would hurry to Jerusalem with the first yield of fruits and beasts, the tithe of cattle and the sheep's first shearings.

I would give these to the priests, the sons of Aaron, for the altar. To the Levites ministering at Jerusalem, I would give my tithe of wine and corn, olives, pomegranates and other fruits. Six years in succession I took the second tithe in money and went and paid it annually at Jerusalem.

I gave the third to orphans and widows and to the strangers who live among the Israelites; I brought it to them as a gift every three years. When we ate, we obeyed both the ordinances of the Law of Moses and the exhortations of Deborah the mother of our ancestor Ananiel; for my father had died and left me an orphan.

(Tobit 1:6-8, *The New Jerusalem Bible*)

By doing some simple addition, you will discover a pattern of giving that may have been overwhelming to most early Christians: for six consecutive years, 10 percent is given to the Levites, or priests; the first and second years of the cycle, another 10 percent is given for the feast; the third year includes 10 percent to widows and orphans; years four and five correspond to years one and two; year six commands fully 30 percent! The yearly average is about 20 percent per year—and disciplined Jews participated!

Tithing was obviously a requirement in the Old Testament. Failure to tithe constituted disobedience to the Law. Malachi 3:6-12 reminds the people that their unwillingness to tithe is tantamount to cheating God. The Lord then challenges them to bring their tithes into the storehouse, and in turn, blesses them abundantly.

The New Testament Tradition

Whereas the regulations governing the tithe are variously articulated in the Old Testament, the New Testament makes little mention of it. Many modern Christians interpret this silence to indicate that persons no longer felt obligated to abide by the Mosaic Law. However, Jesus' speech in the Sermon on the Mount makes clear that he has not come to abolish the Law but to fulfill it (Matt. 5:17). In other words, one can argue that Jesus did not mention the tithe because faithful Jews already adhered to the laws concerning it. Any religious Jew would know and practice this duty. Luke 11:42 lends support to this view when Jesus condemns the Pharisees, not because they have tithed, but because they have neglected "justice and the love of God." The two themes Jesus emphasized most often related to the reign of God and to persons' attitudes about their possessions. The Pharisees tithed, but their relationships and attitudes were far removed.

A defensible argument either for or against the tithe cannot be made on the basis of the scanty evidence of Jesus' comments on tithing. However, a look at what Jesus had to say about stewardship will enable us to set tithing within a broader context.

Jesus' parable of the faithful and unfaithful servants is recorded in Luke 12:41-48 and Matthew 24:45-51. The steward is one who has been entrusted to care for the resources of the owner. In fact, the word *steward* means "overseer of a household." The crucial point is that stewards do not own the resources. God is the owner, for "the earth is the Lord's and the fullness thereof" (Ps. 24:1). Stewards are expected to care for the owner's property in a responsible manner. Those stewards who prove to be faithful managers of a small amount will be given more to control. In contrast, stewards who abuse the property, thereby showing themselves to be untrustworthy, will be punished by the Master.

Similarly, the recipients of the talents in another parable were to be stewards of the money that their master entrusts to them (Matt. 25:14-30). The money was not theirs but his. When the owner returns from his journey, he calls the three stewards to give an account of their administration of his money. Careful management enabled two of the three to report a substantial profit. The third man had *buried* the money in the ground. Hidden money is dead money. There is *no* possibility for growth, change, or increase. The owner was angry with this steward who was so unfaithful that he had not even deposited the talent in the bank to earn interest. As was true in the previous parable, those stewards who proved themselves to be faithful with small amounts were given greater resources to oversee. From those who have a lot, a great deal is expected!

In these two parables, Jesus emphasizes the ownership of God and the faithfulness of the stewards assigned to oversee God's property. The stewards did not simply consider 10 percent of what they had to be God's, but all of it. A willingness to give, to trust that *all* is God's, makes a difference. Are we able to offer to God what has always been and always will be God's? Is our primary relationship with God? *Is* God first in our lives? Jesus affirms this understanding of stewardship when he commends the widow who gave all that she had to God (Luke 21:1-4).

Like Jesus, Paul does not speak about contributing a tenth. Giving was neither restricted to a tithe nor to be done out of a sense of obligation and duty. Instead, Paul praises the Macedonians who gave "beyond their means, of their own free will" (2 Cor. 8:1-6). Their joy in the Lord was reflected in their sacrificial giving to help other people. Paul understands Jesus' teaching that a person's sense of well-being does not increase along with material possessions and comforts. Paul encourages people to carry money lightly to use it to accomplish God's work, and to avoid bondage to it (Phil. 4:12).

The importance of the giver's attitude toward giving is also highlighted in 2 Corinthians 9:7-10. The one who gives cheerfully, "as he has made up his mind," will be cared for by God. Paul's emphasis on liberal offering indicates that Christians are to give bountifully. They are also to give on a systematic basis, for Paul instructs the church at Corinth to collect contributions "on the first day of every week" (1 Cor. 16:1-3).

Members of the New Testament church committed themselves and the resources they controlled unto God. Their giving stemmed from a sense of joy in God's inexpressible gift of Jesus Christ. Their zeal for their faith and willingness to risk persecution for the cause of Christ surely would have resulted in gifts that at least matched—and most likely exceeded—the Old Testament standard of a tithe.

The Church Tradition

Throughout the course of Christian church history, beginning with Constantine in the fourth century, church and state are often closely intertwined. If the ruling monarch accepted Christ, then the region and its inhabitants became Christian. Tithes or taxes were collected to support these government-established churches. Persons were expected to contribute, whether they believed in Jesus Christ or not. In the

Church of England, for example, the people were taxed by the state, and the clergy and churches were supported out of these collections. To this day, the clergy are supported by all citizens born naturally into the Church of England.

Prior to the acceptance of the United States Constitution, some colonies had churches funded by the populace. After the Constitution guaranteed the separation of church and state, churches were disestablished from the state and had to rely on voluntary support. Consequently, tithing was encouraged to underwrite the cost of maintaining the congregation. In some churches, tithing was a requirement of church membership.

During the rapid industrial expansion of the nineteenth century, tithing was touted as a sound investment. Christian tithers would be blessed by God, who would pour out riches from the storehouse. Therefore, tithing was seen by some persons as a way to multiply their assets.

Today, some U.S. churches still strongly proclaim the blessing of tithing. Most Christian congregations, however, resort to fund-raising techniques that emphasize the needs of the church budget, rather than the opportunity to make a response to God through the commitment of at least a tithe. Consequently, tithers constitute a small minority of Christians. In many instances, church members are unaware that tithing is a *spiritual* discipline. The issues of money and giving are taboo—we are unwilling to accept that giving brings to money the power of grace!

The Motivation for Giving

As we examine these ideas, it is clear that no one formula for giving has been used consistently throughout Judeo-Christian history. It is equally clear that even when people give a tenth, their motivations for doing so vary greatly. The effect upon the giver is quite different, depending upon whether the tithe is seen as a duty to the law, an obligation to a state church, a means to amass greater wealth, or a joyous response to God's gracious love.

The Jews were required by law to give a tenth, though when one considers the varieties of tithes called for in the Pentateuch, it appears that 10 percent was a minimum. During some years after the exile that figure was as high as 20 or 30 percent. (Refer to Tobit 1:6-8.) Because upholding the law was of paramount importance to the devout Jew, the giving of the tithe was crucial.

Committed Christians of the early church apparently did not limit themselves to 10 percent. Instead, they were motivated to give not by the law but by their own feelings of gratitude for God's love as expressed in Jesus. They gave a portion of their resources, recognizing God's ownership of all things and their stewardship of those things.

Later in church history, whenever the tithe was a requirement of the government to support a state church, it was imposed on all persons living within the area. Surely, a non-believer or marginally committed Christian would have resented the tithe, for it was not a gift but a tax, not an acknowledgment that God is the owner of all creation but a burden to be borne.

The motivation of the nineteenth-century American, especially the entrepreneur, for giving a tithe differed still. Rather than seeing the tithe as a legal requirement, a state tax, or an opportunity to return a portion of God's bounty, business persons saw the tithe as a good investment. They reasoned, "If I give a tithe, the Lord will bless me and enable my enterprise to flourish." To give in this manner does not require that one recognize God as the owner of all things. Indeed, this idea would have been difficult to consider, for it would have clashed with that of the rugged individualist, the totally self-reliant person.

The Tithe as a Symbolic Response

These different interpretations of and motivations for tithing perhaps inadvertently cause much confusion for modern Christians. In some churches the very mention of "tithing" raises voices against legalism. The idea of returning to God that which is God's is foreign to persons who believe they are owners, not stewards, of what they have. Persons who perceive themselves as owners base their giving on fiscal criteria, not spiritual ones.

Where do we as modern Christian disciples who want to be faithful to God stand in relation to the tithe? As we begin to understand our role as stewards, we recognize that God owns everything. Then we realize that the tithe is only a symbol which becomes a minimum offering, rather than an absolute figure. We also take care to be good stewards of the other 90 percent of the resources entrusted to us by God to oversee.

The decision to tithe must be a spiritual one rather than financial! There is a difference between spiritual math and secular math: when I *spend* $10.00 of the $100.00 that I possess, that $10.00 is gone. I must do the best I can with $90.00. When I *give* $10.00 to God through the church, that $10.00 is God's will alive in the world. Then, God and I *together* are doing the best that can be done with the remaining $90.00.

For Christians who view tithing within the work of God's law and God's grace, the giving of a tenth of one's income becomes a joyous act of worship. Our tithe is just one way to express our love and gratitude to the God who is not only sovereign of the universe but our closest friend.

Nan Duerling, Ph.D.
Crownsville, Maryland

PART 2
Personal Responses

Each of us is witness to our own story, our personal journey with God. Feelings about the experiences with tithing are a part of the tale. Here are some reflections by people in various stages of growth who agreed to share parts of their stories.

As you read their words, listen with your heart and with a willing spirit. You *may* laugh, weep, disagree, rejoice—you *will* be blessed.

Norma W. Wimberly
Nashville, Tennessee

Tithing is an important part of a Christian's life. The Bible tells us that we should tithe, and thus it is a practice that all Christians should follow. Tithing also provides us with a chance to show God that we are thankful for what we have and to share our resources with others. God has given us so much, and tithing is one way that we can give back unto the Lord part of what is God's. Tithing also shows a commitment to serving the Lord, thus we can feel good about ourselves as well as please God. Given out of love and care, tithing should be a fulfilling experience, not a burdensome duty. When we tithe, we just need to remember that we are serving and pleasing God, for "God loves a cheerful giver" (2 Cor. 9:7).

Jim Norris
Brentwood, Tennessee

My wife, Barbara, and I started tithing in 1955 and consider it the most significant decision we have made in our marriage because of the life-improving changes and blessings that have taken place since that time. Because I was a tither, I was offered a position as a professional church fund-raiser and later became the volunteer Director of Stewardship for the then Southern-California-Arizona Annual Conference of The United Methodist Church, and a member of the National Association of Stewardship Leaders for ten years.

The greatest revelation I ever received about tithing and its importance happened several years ago when I was preparing for a stewardship seminar. I was using The Living Bible to refresh my memory about the three kinds of tithes mentioned in Numbers and Deuteronomy. When I read Deuteronomy 14:23c, this paraphrased version says that "God gave us tithing to teach us to put Him first in our lives."

Literally the Bible says that we learn to fear the Lord our God everyday, which is another way of saying that the tithe will help us put God first.

Suddenly it became clear why God had included tithing in the Law. He was giving the Jews (and us) a tool to help us overcome Mammon and live by the first commandment. We now had a method by which we could achieve the most difficult goal we have to face—putting our trust in the Almighty God instead of the Almighty dollar! This made it even more clear why the decision to tithe is a spiritual decision and not a financial one.

If putting God first in our lives is the most important thing we have to do, and tithing will teach us how to do this, then tithing is an absolute necessity for each and every one of us who claims to be Christian.

Ray E. Van Alstine
Lakewood, California

I did not grow up a tither. As I prepared to serve my first charge full time, my wife and I decided to "try" tithing. We have discovered that giving back to God the first 10 percent of monies entrusted to us has not made us "poorer"; we have been enriched in many ways. It is possible to tithe. You can do it too!

Terry W. Allen
Detroit, Michigan

We have not always tithed but felt that we should. We tried to figure on paper how we could do this but could not come up with the extra money. Finally we just decided to give it a try to see what would happen. We were surprised to find that we got all of our bills paid and even had a little left. We have made it a habit ever since.

Sandy Eddy

I began to try to tithe in a seminary out of a deep sense of guilt. Tithing was something you were supposed to do. My first attempts were dismal. We would pay our bills and by the end of the month, there wasn't enough left to give God 10 percent. We actually kept a record of our debt to God. As that grew, we became more and more dejected. Then one day I was at a friend's home as he was opening his mail. He received a large refund check from an insurance company, completely unexpectedly. He was ecstatic, because after paying his bills, he had only had fifty dollars to get through the month. I began to share about our difficulties with tithing. My friend shared two principles which completely transformed our giving. First, he pointed out that my giving experience was not joyful. God wants us to give willingly out of a feeling of appreciation, and thanksgiving, not as a qualification for sainthood. Secondly, what we desire to give to God should be from our first fruits. The first check he wrote every month was to the church. Following this plan, we first dropped the 10 percent figure to one we could manage more successfully, given our limited income, and then we wrote the church's check first. It didn't take long, however, before we realized we could give 10 percent. Giving to the church first increased our giving and has made tithing exciting.

Lane Bailey
Prairie Village, Kansas

When I worked as a church secretary-youth director forty years ago and earned $1,800 a year, I probably tithed. After that two-year interlude, I married a non-church affiliate. He is a fine person, but his commitment to the church is not such that he would choose tithing in the restricted sense. Of course, I switched vocations and no longer received pay for serving the church and community. I have been happy being able to share freely with others.

If tithing means giving a tenth of one's pre-tax income to the church, then I must admit, "We don't qualify." I say "we" because my husband and I are a team. What we have is "ours," not "his" or "hers."

Yes, I believe God is Creator, Father, and Giver of All! In return for the gift of life, I want to show my gratitude by being a responsible steward. I must care for my whole body—a temple of God, my family, my church, my community, and my environment. I must plan, use, and share my talents and resources wisely. Contrary to the Scripture that admonishes

"Take no thought for the morrow," I think it judicious to provide not only for the children's college education, but also for those retirement years which are growing in number for so many people.

Having professed this credo, why do we not give more?

Knowing that the government, using nearly half of our personal income, does many benevolent deeds for others (welfare, education, medicare, and certain kinds of foreign aid, all items for which the church used to be more responsible), we feel that we are helping others. Of course we give additional support to the church, the United Way fund, colleges, the arts, and a host of other good causes, more than 10 percent of the after-tax figure.

We love our God. We love His people. We want to help them. God has been very good to us. We want to share His generosity with others! May we continue to grow in our willingness to help carry another's burden and to bear witness to a song of hope.

Ruth Blair
Midland, Michigan

My wife, Katherine, and I started tithing with our first paycheck after we were married. We have tithed for thirty-three years, very happy years. God has blessed us so much. Tithing is one way we can show our gratitude for the abundance and grace which God bestows upon us each day.

Paul Raby
Asheville, North Carolina

Tithing deepens the faith of the tither, as any who tithe understand. If we wait until we can "afford" to tithe, we probably never will. But if our tithing grows out of genuine thanksgiving, that disciplined act has a way of putting all our values into perspective.

Tithing is also contagious. I know this because the giving/sharing pattern in our family has grown significantly as we have been inspired by the witness of tithers, gladly attesting to the joys it brings into their lives.

A good friend of mine came to me as his pastor for help in a time of turmoil. He had recently moved with his family into a large new home. That move, combined with all of the lures of affluent living, soon put my friend deeper into debt than he had ever been. That debt was overwhelming him, and he found himself taking out his desperation on his family, rather than sharing his considerable concern with them.

He poured out his anguish, and shared how, in struggling with this problem, he had come to a renewed appreciation of how important his marriage and family were to him. He feared the damage he had done them.

Together, we were able to see the strength he had in his family, and the wisdom of sharing this problem with his wife, rather than shielding her. He felt confident as we parted. Not long afterward, my friend took me aside. "Things are better than I ever dared hope," he told me. "We are working our way out, and we'll make it!"

Then he added, "We are so grateul for all that we do have that we have decided to tithe, starting the first of the year. But we don't want anyone to know!"

I affirmed the peace and joy that had come to my friend, but I added, "When you get into tithing, and experience the blessings that will overflow in your life, you are going to have to talk about it! Such experience will be too good to keep to yourself!"

That is an observation, born out of my own experience, of what happens with all who tithe!

George Englehardt
Cheshire, Connecticut

As a Christian, I believe that I owe all that I have to our Heavenly Father who gave his only Son for my salvation. Thus, both through creation and redemption, supreme love was manifested toward me. I feel that tithing is only a first response in recognizing that all of my blessings come from my Heavenly Father and his dear Son. While tithing and additional freewill offerings have been a part of my life since my earliest years, I cannot repay in any way the sacrifice made for me. In fact, tithing is not something I give to God, but an additional blessing God gives to me.

G. Tom Carter
Washington, DC

Somewhere along the way, I have gained a sense that the "tithe" involves much more than money or material gifts of any kind. Cain seems to have given the proper amount, but in the wrong spirit. I cannot attach a specific percentage even to the money aspect. The Old Testament gives 10 percent as a minimum, but that legalistic amount might be given out of obligation and not love. Tithing is a way of life that causes a person to respond to God's love by giving as much of one's self as possible at a given time. To say that it only requires 10 percent would allow you to "pay up" and feel that you were debt-free. We can never repay a debt that involves a gift as large as God has given. To take this one step further, I cannot even give out of a sense of debt because Jesus paid the debt. I can only give from a sense of love which has no bounds. Certainly, 10 percent would be too small a price to put on this love. The way I use my life and all its resources is the only way to judge my tithe.

Pat Stroman
Waco, Texas

Yes, I tithe! It has been a question for me. When our children were small, my husband suggested we tithe. My first question was, "How will we pay our bills?"

I had some very large medical bills, and my husband's salary as a young Methodist clergyman wasn't large. How would we buy what we needed for the children? But, trusting in my husband's good judgment and believing in the Scriptures, we began. I soon learned that taking the tithe off the top meant we had to budget. I also learned we always had what we *needed*, but not necessarily what we *wanted!*

It became a joy to see what the Lord wanted us to do next. Because of part of our tithe we went to Japan to teach for two months. We saw young people go to college and seminary. The Asian Rural Institute in Japan sent out another student to teach better training methods. Habitat for Humanity built another home for a low-income family.

I am not a generous person by nature but I became more generous, more giving, when I developed a plan for giving.

We spent our early years developing a plan (educating ourselves) for earning. Then, along the way, we learned to develop a plan for saving and spending. Almost never are we helped to develop a plan for giving. Someone once suggested that we ought to develop a giving plan first, just because our natural tendency is toward selfishness.

That, of course, is what Scripture offers us when it speaks of the tithe or a proportion. (Somehow this message doesn't seem to get through to us—probably because it is rarely taught.) The tithe is really a plan for giving which says to decide what you want to give and give it off the top.

That is the key to finding joy in giving. For years I never found much joy in giving. All the requests that came along often irritated me. They seemed to be trying to take something away from me. Then I made the decision to tithe, though it took a few years to work up to it—one or two percentage points a year.

Once I had made the decision on a percentage I wanted to give, joy began to come into my giving. Giving became a positive adventure in my life. As I made my offering on Sunday morning, I could rejoice in the good our church was doing. When other requests come in, I am able to consider them on their merits—not "can we afford it"—the money is already there. I have come to expect this money to be the "best investment" I make.

Our children are on their own now. They tithe because of the example that was set in their home.

Joan Gelhaus
Sun Prairie, Wisconsin

Many, many times I have put the scriptural promise, "Prove me now in this," says the Lord of hosts. . . .(Mal. 3:10), *to a test.* In essence, I was saying, "God, show me that you are faithful to your promise."

I felt the need to give at least one-tenth of my income to the ministry, even through the very lean years of my life. As a widow with three small children, God remained my constant source. My rationale remains, "If God can provide for the little sparrow, surely God can provide for my needs." Sometimes, I even get some of my "wants."

Over and over again, doors have been opened, ways have been made, and needs have been met. I'm now convinced—you can't beat God-giving. The more you give, the more God gives to you. I challenge others to "try God."

Mary Boyd
Nashville, Tennessee

C. J. is now seventy years young. He and his wife of forty-nine years are "tithers and proud of it." His story is one of faithfulness, struggles, and joy.

C. J. says, "We made a decision to try tithing when we were just newlyweds. Both of us had been raised in the church and had been taught about giving and tithing since we were children. I was making $92.00 per month at the time and every time we got paid we would sit down and take out the 10 percent for the church. I wish that I could say that we always did that but there were times when other things took precedence over the Lord. We always managed to come back to the tithe, though. We just felt that was the right thing to do."

"I've been retired about four years now, and tithing is more important than ever. We can't give nearly as much as we used to, but we know that as long as we are giving the Lord his 10 percent, then we are doing our share. We feel good about that."

"I want to say one more thing. The struggles to be tithers were as important as the giving. In those struggles we grew in the faith and as husband and wife. The experience is not just giving 10 percent but what it takes to get there. . . . Tithing has blessed us in so many ways. We have received much more than we have given."

Roy Stephenson
Jackson, Tennessee

There are many people who influence us in all areas of our lives. In mine, when it came to the church and money—it was my parents. Those people loved to give money (and talents) to Glencoe, Alabama, First Church. Three times they were audited by Uncle Sam and his "boys." Even though there were the cancelled checks to prove it, they would not allow for "that" much giving to a little local church. No sir (no Ma'am), they just wouldn't allow it—they said nobody gives that much to the church!

A lot of this was bound to rub off on me (and my sister) and it did, even though sometimes the budget is tight and it's tough to give. But, I figure if I can afford my VCR, my bassboat, my hunting club dues, and my yearly trips to Gatlinburg, I can give God his due—I just wish I could give more.

Charles Wells
Andrews, South Carolina

During the course of my life and my relationship with God, I have been a single person, a parent in the traditional nuclear family, a single parent, and single once again. During that time I have struggled with my finances, my responsibility to myself, my community, my family, and my church. It has not always been easy to set aside money for God's work.

Since youth my parents trained me to be a tither. If I earned fifty cents, five was put away for God's work through the church. Anything that I wanted to give in the community was separate from what was always considered God's money. I have carried that philosophy to adulthood. I do not see the tithe as "good works used for both the church and the community." I see it as my response to God's blessings in my life to be sent back through the church. My response to community appeals and community charity is out of the other portion of my income. God has uniquely blessed me and sustained me through life, and I respond to that message with a tithe to the church.

Gwendolyn J. Myers
Overland Park, Kansas

Personally, I cannot remember a time when I have not been exposed to the discipline of tithing. As a child, I can remember my father placing my allowance of fifty cents in my hand then reminding me that a nickel belonged to Jesus. As I grew older, I continued to contribute 10 percent of my income to the church.

However, it has only been in the last few years that the power of tithing has made a difference in our family life. With three growing children and an ever-increasingly expensive economy, it is more and more tempting to think of what that extra 10 percent could buy. But, that 10 percent is God's. It is my statement of faith that the values, morals, and ethics of God's love and forgiveness and renewal are true and that the church is God's principle agent of spiritual transformation to bring peace and hope in our world. I put my money where my heart is.

Tithing is a part of my witness that all of my life is Christ's. I read the Scriptures as a spiritual discipline and a statement of faith that my mind and thoughts are God's. I pray as a spiritual discipline and a statement of faith that my inner thoughts, feelings, ambitions, hopes, doubts, and fears are God's. I attend church as a spiritual discipline and a statement of faith that I am a part of the household of the faithful and we are God's children. I serve others as a spiritual discipline and a statement of faith that good works and faith go together. I tithe my income as a spiritual discipline and a statement of faith that this world and all that is in it is God's. I am called to glorify God with my stewardship of what I have received.

I wish for everyone the opportunity to grow in God's grace and firmly believe that one discipline that enables that growth is tithing

Davis Thompson
Nashville, Arkansas

John M. Templeton, founder of the Templeton group of mutual funds, concluded a speech to the International Association for Financial Planning by confiding that he had been asked by a financial planner at the convention to mention the name of the "very best opportunity" for investing in the world today.

"I told him that the most risk-free investment, the most rewarding investment was tithing . . . It means giving 10 percent of your income to your church and charities. In my forty-six years of experience, I have never known anyone who regretted that investment. I have never known anyone who has made that investment for ten years without being rewarded with both happiness and prosperity."

Once, when I was part of an every member visitation team, a man told me he couldn't afford to tithe. I told him I couldn't afford *not* to!

When I was younger and just starting in business—seventy-three miles away from the little church where I grew up—a local business man came to visit me. This man was a pillar of the church, and well-known in the community for spectacular business deals. This unlikely person helped me to begin to see and understand the blessing and spiritual growth from generous giving. Maybe I didn't admire his business activities, but he left me with the gift of being a tither.

Jackson Miller
Altoona, Pennsylvania

I firmly believe money isn't everything in life. I also believe that the more you give, the richer you are. That's been true in our family, with the blessings which have proven our richness over and over in times of love and sorrow.

I find myself, even today, supporting not one but several churches and their events, plus other worthwhile organizations. If I had not had the faith in God that I have had during my entire life journey, I honestly don't know where I'd be today. Each day I let the "good book" speak through me as I search for answers and pray that God will forgive us and will continue watching over all of us.

You see, money isn't the most important concern. It is loving and caring for one another and taking the time to listen to one another that matters. Tithing is important, but faith, trust, and love are essential.

Marie Vinsonhaler
Lincoln, Nebraska

What giving my tithe means to me: I can help someone else to know my Lord and Savior Jesus Christ as their *personal Savior.* I can have a part in seeing many grow by practicing God's Word, fellowshiping with others, and being happy to say, "This is where I *get* to worship my Lord."

What giving my offering means to me: I can give over and above my tithe to bring LOVE to others.

Clara Bass
Foley, Missouri

In short, tithing is a way to take control over your money, and so over your life. It gives you a chance to look at your whole getting and spending picture; to explore simpler living; to laugh, love, and praise God. It helps to meditate often on 2 Corinthians 9.

Matthew Gates
Osterville, Massachusetts

It was always a joy to give gifts to my loved ones . . . my wife, my children and their wives, my grandchildren, special friends and relatives . . . but I was uncomfortable when it came time to give my gift (was it too little? too much? adequate?) to the Lord. Then, I gave my life to Jesus Christ to use as he desired and that problem disappeared; tithing became a conversion experience and a way of life.

Now, giving to my Lord is not a duty but a privilege and a joy. The more I give, the more God gives to me. It's a never-ending cycle.

Thanks be to God, Hallelujah!

Bob Smythe
Nashville, Tennessee

I personally have struggled with tithing. I once lived in a household whose income was three times what mine is now. I never came close to tithing. I thought about it, but I just didn't think I could. It was during seminary when I was making $5,000 a year that I began to tithe.

Tithing for me has become a spiritual discipline, not a financial responsibility. There is something about being committed to giving that has helped me realize that my faith is in God, not in my ability to purchase goods and services.

Over and over this week, I have been reading the Timothy Scripture (2 Tim. 4:3-5). The author clearly presents guidelines for ministry. In some ways my itching ears want to say, "Whatever you give is okay or you can do as you please with your life." That would, as the writer of Timothy says, "cure the itching ear." Yet that seems to support the popular myth that we live in a vacuum and are not interconnected to others. Each of us has gifts that come because God has freely given to us. The talents, the energy, the time, the commitment, and the money that we give back to God are gifts which we . . . have vowed to share. Many have heard the saying "Give until it hurts"; I detest that saying. What God wants for us is the best—not hurt. I think a better saying is "Give until it feels healthy." Spiritual healthiness is multifaceted. As you attend meetings and make prayerful decisions about gift-giving to the Body of Christ, explore the possibility of tithing as a once and for all cure for itching ears.

The Reverend Eva K. Brown
Topeka, Kansas

Giving is one of the most visible attributes of Korean people. Emotional attachment among neighbors, and fellowship out of that kind of relationship, has existed in the history of Korean people for many centuries. Koreans are people who love to give something away. Many Westerners who visit the country often comment that Koreans are extraordinary people who are concerned about their neighbors and even strangers. This "extra" thing, according to a Western standard, causes some kind of uncomfortable feeling, but it has long been a part of their identity.

Accepting Jesus as Lord always has a strong association with the question, "How do I give in response to the event of the crucifixion?" The concept of a "free gift" does not work well among Korean people. It is not to say that they do not know the countless grace of God shown on the cross, but somehow it is not possible for them to be "free receivers."

Tithing is not as remote here as in the States. Indeed, tithing is expected, and those who belong to a Christian church in Korea are committed to tithing. For example, a church my father founded and served for more than twenty years has more than 75 percent members who tithe out of about ten thousand total membership. It is amazing what the church can do with that kind of commitment and dedication. Even though enthusiasm and a sense of responsibility are reduced in the States, Korean immigrant Christians are still carrying the theology and commitment they had in their homeland. By considering the size and history of their churches, it has been amazing to see their growth and plan for the future.

I am glad that I serve both English- and Korean-speaking congregations in real ways, for that special way of serving brought me into a full understanding of how they were and are, and of potential communication with English congregations about this critical aspect of Christian faith.

Cheol Hwan Kwak
Korea

I have noticed that persons who tithe are happy people. In fact, as recently as last January one man told me that after twenty-six years of difficulties and unhappiness, he began to tithe, and since then his life has been fuller, richer, and happier. Another man had a most successful year in business, but somehow he felt no sense of accomplishment and fulfillment. When the time came to do his income tax return, he realized his income had increased many times that year, but his giving to the church had not changed! He took immediate steps to remedy that situation and found peace and a sense of worth once more. I have one concern, which I discovered through my journey with Ventures in Mission: There are people with a lot of assets (e.g., land and buildings) whose income is relatively low. If they tithe, it is based on their income, not all of their treasures. I wonder if that is an honest approach to tithing?

My understanding has been that tithing is what I give to the poor; I give to the church over and above that!

Margot Ball
Toronto, Ontario

PART 3
Personal Meditation

J ournaling has been called "another door to God's presence." Most of us know that good stewards and managers keep good records. A record—a journal—of spiritual growth and change is good stewardship and can lead us to a closer relationship with God. Some people use their journals to reflect on daily life events, meditate on the scriptures, record dreams, goals, and ideas, or respond to quotes and conversations.

You are invited to establish a daily discipline of personal reading, reflection, and meditation for fourteen days. Here are suggestions for that time alone with God, references to scripture passages related to tithing, and space for you to reflect on your response to God.

There is no "right way." Sacred and holy times and places can be anywhere, any time. I pray that you will accept space and time as another of God's gifts and open yourself to God. Spiritual disciplines are formative and lead to freedom. In solitude with God, we establish and maintain the vital, life-giving relationship that enables us *to be* who God intends us to be and *to do* what God intends us to do.

Reading, studying, and experiencing the scriptures are ways of listening to God. God's message is communicated through happenings, frequently in an unexpected conflict of wills—ours vs. God's. Hearing God is a dynamic process of information and formation, and ongoing relationship. Each of us becomes a new person, shaped by God's Word. Read the suggested scriptural passages carefully. Offer your reflections to God for God to use in your life. Listen and wait; then respond to God with gratitude and joy.

Day One

Read Genesis 28:10-22.

Give a few moments to imagine Jacob on his journey, to feel the holiness of the place where he dreamed, to see the altar at Bethel, and to remember Jacob's promise to God.

Now reflect upon your journey of faith. Describe some of the places you have felt God's presence, some of the ways you have worshiped, some of your vows to God. Tell your story. Where is *your* Bethel?

Day Two

Read Psalm 24:1-6.

God is the God of *all* creation. God is with *you*. Jacob came into the presence of God in a state of inspired prayer. He expected God's best for him and offered his best to God. When *we* pray, shouldn't we offer *our* best—whether we pray at an altar of stone, kneel on new grass, or sit in a church?

Write and pray a prayer, offering your best to God today, expecting God's best for you.

Day Three

Read Numbers 18:25-27.

Moses was a stuttering shepherd with a history of adventure, coincidence, and miracles. From his rescue by Pharaoh's daughter to meeting God at a burning bush through leading the people of Israel from bondage in Egypt, there was *God's* order to his life. God continues, in the scripture passage, to alert Moses to the order of life lived in relationship to God.

What is the order of your life? Outline your plans for today. What do your plans reveal about God's intention for you and your growing relationship to God?

Sit quietly and listen to God's presence. Pray for *God's* order in your plans for today. Write down any changes you could make.

Day Four

Read Psalm 145:15-16.

Giving begins with God, continues with God, always extends from God. God is giving to you now—enough and more to satisfy your needs. Make a list of blessings, a gratitude list with at *least twenty* entries—the wealth of your life. Be specific! Was it hard to list twenty?

Day Five

Read Deuteronomy 14:22-29.

Sharing a meal with others is a part of God's intention for God's children. Be still and imagine a feast such as the Israelites may have enjoyed as they worshiped the Lord. Remember the joy of Holy Communion. Reflect upon a time of celebration with family or friends when food was shared.

Today, you will eat. List here in a column some of the food items that may be a part of your food plan. In a second column adjacent to the first repeat each item. Place a one (1) before each food listed in the first column; place a nine (9) before each food listed in the second column. Imagine that the first list is God's table (a tithe), the second is yours. See how bountiful your table is!

Pray that today you will remember how God is blessing you. Are you putting *God* first in your life? God gives to you. How do *you* give to God?

Day Six

Read Micah 6:6-8.

Micah's prophecy asks questions concerning a person's relationship with God, with possessions, and with other people. The questions are answered with the call *to do, to show, to live,* and *to love.*

Describe a healthy, loving relationship you share with another person. What visible actions do you take to establish and maintain that relationship?

Describe what you believe is a healthy, loving relationship with God. What visible actions do you take to establish and maintain that relationship?

What could you do differently to enable your relationship with God and other people to grow?

Day Seven

Read Deuteronomy 26:11-13.

Begin your time of meditation in prayer. Feel the gratitude you have for the good things the Lord has given you, your family, and your friends. Remind yourself that gratitude is a gift of grace. Recognizing and accepting grace moves us into an ever closer relationship with God.

List here some of the relationships and experiences for which you are grateful. In an additional adjacent column, list some of the actions you take as a result of your gratitude. What action(s) do you or can you take because of your fuller relationship with God? Remember that *listening* to God helps us *know* God. Knowledge leads to action.

Day Eight

Read 2 Corinthians 9:7-10.

Loving is not the result of regret, guilt, duty, or obligation. Love is glad, generous, and given freely and abundantly. Generous, glad love grows and lasts.

Sometimes, though, people and circumstances change, and something may interfere with a loving relationship. For a few minutes, close your eyes and quietly reflect on what may have gotten in the way between you and God. After your reflection, pray for the courage of honesty to list those things. Has it been a selfish attitude or an unhealthy relationship with money, or other people? After you compile your list, release it into God's hands. Thank God for providing all you need.

Day Nine

Read Malachi 3:6-12.

You change, people change, circumstances change—but God does not change. In the passage from Malachi, we are reminded that we sometimes rob ourselves of a full, rich, intimate, honest relationship with God.

Pray for God's forgiveness. Knowing you are forgiven and loved, reflect on the concept of tithing as a tool, a habit that God uses to mend our hearts. Tithing is a remedy for a spiritual disease that afflicts the human soul—a possessive heart.

Write a letter to God revealing how you feel about living in a loving, trusting relationship with God. Include how you feel about tithing.

Day Ten

Read Mark 12:38-44.

Do you know someone who has the type of relationship with God that the widow had? How does the person you know manifest a love of heart, mind, soul, and strength on a daily basis? Describe here the characteristics and attributes of this person.

Call this person and make an appointment to talk about this individual's relationship with God. Make a covenant with yourself to discuss tithing as a part of your visit. You may feel a little uncomfortable about the call. Trust that the person whom you will visit will feel honored.

Day Eleven

Read Luke 11:42 and Matthew 23:25-28.

The Pharisees had a problem—their actions were merely functional, not a response to an intimate relationship with God. They felt that their *doing* guaranteed the quality of *being* that God expected.

Reflect for a while on the quality of your *being*, your inner health. How is it shown in your actions? Are you just looking good, or are you being real? Does your love for God *show*? How?

Day Twelve

Read Hebrews 7:1-10.

The Good News of the Son of God involves not only *God's action* on our behalf, but our *active response* to God. We are called into God's fellowship, as was our father Abraham; we are commissioned to serve God, just as our brother Paul; we are given special responsibilities. We have an exciting history whereby we see others putting God first. Do we?

Write a letter to an imaginary ancestor in which you ask questions about that individual's values, actions, and way of putting God first. Search your heart and mind for whatever glimmer of doubt may make you feel uncomfortable with generous giving through tithing. Tell your imaginary ancestor how you feel. Ask the hard questions of faith.

Day Thirteen

Read 2 Chronicles 31:4-10.

The people living in Jerusalem gave abundantly and devoted themselves to the Lord. The passage from 2 Chronicles emphasizes generosity in graphic words: "great amounts," "piled in heaps," "enough and
to spare." The images are not those of burdensome duty, but a praise,
blessing, joyful celebration—a party! Because the people had a relationship with God *first,* there were blessings and leftovers.

Quietly pray and think back over the past twelve days of this part of
your journey of faith. What growth do you see? Briefly outline the days,
and note times of new insight and closeness to God, as well as times of
doubt when you found yourself moving away from God.

Day Fourteen

Read John 3:16-18.

God gave and continues to give. Nothing came between the relationship of God and Jesus, the only child. Each of us is an only child! Jesus surrendered heart, strength, mind, and soul to God. Because of Jesus' *consciousness* of God, each moment was a sign of *action with God*.

W. Paul Jones (St. Paul School of Theology, Kansas City, Missouri) has written, "What more does the Incarnation declare than God's promise that we are in it together?" Tithing is one way to trust in God's love, providence, and constant care. It is an action, a tool, an outward and visible sign of an inward and spiritual grace.

Read and reflect upon the following prayer of response.

A Prayer of Response

Gracious God:

Jesus Christ made it possible for You to be our God and for us to be Your people.

You are my God, and I am Your person.

But You require that there are to be no Gods before You. You are to be first in my life.

But Lord I find that that is almost impossible.

Something or someone always seems to be in the way. Or maybe just as Adam and Eve, I want to be God myself.

But God, You have given me a way to learn how to put You first in my life.

You have given me tithing, and You have said that if I will tithe, You will pour upon me an overflowing blessing.

You have said to put You to the test.

I believe You, Lord, and I want to be blessed by You, both with a greater faith and with a more abundant life.

So, starting today, God, and for the next thirty days, I am going to give You the first fruits of my life, the first tenth of all I receive, and have the faith that all You have promised will come true.

I make this pledge and prayer in the sacred name of Your Son, our Lord and Savior, Jesus Christ, and I thank You now for the blessings I am about to receive. Amen and Amen.

Ray E. Van Alstine

Read the prayer again. Pray for guidance in the coming thirty days of *your* life, as you respond to God in all of your loving, growing, living, and giving.

Write your own prayer as a reminder of these two weeks of decisive response. Pray for willingness and release into freedom with God. Be still and know God.

PART 4
Group Study Guide

To the Leader

You have chosen to explore the spiritual adventure of tithing. You may or may not presently tithe. The group of people who will share with you in these four sessions may or may not tithe. Remember that each individual is searching for insight into the scriptures, willing to be guided by Christian traditions, eager to explore new possibilities, and doing enough to share experiences and dreams in a community setting.

This study guide provides an outline for four group sessions. As a leader, you can ensure a time of learning and spiritual growth for your group by following these suggestions:

1. Read carefully and prayerfully the first three sections of this book.

2. Make sure that each person in the study group has a copy of this manual. Encourage each one to commit to fourteen days of personal study and reflection on the scriptures. (See Part 3, "Personal Meditation.")

3. If possible, schedule the four sessions within a fourteen-day, two-week period. In this way, you and each person in the group will experience *personal* growth within the setting of the *community*.

4. Be honest about your own style of leadership. You may feel more comfortable with a lecture method. If so, take time to make notes of what you feel led to say. You may prefer to concentrate on small group discussion. Whatever your choice, take time to know the people in the group. *Their* needs and understandings can help you to be an effective leader. How can you best work together to change lives?

5. Be more interested in *transformation* than information. You do not need to be an expert. The Holy Spirit will be active within the group. Trust in God's power and presence.

Session One: Who? Whose? What?

(Suggested Time: One Hour)

I. Coming Together

   A. Share a prayer of thanksgiving for God's generous giving, for each person in the group, and for the willingness to grow together in faith.

   B. Get acquainted with one another and with the reasons (or spiritual nudges) you are together. Why did you choose to be a part of this study?

   C. Alert the group to the importance of reading, studying, and using this book, not only in group sessions, but as a daily spiritual discipline. Urge the participants to embark on the fourteen-day personal journey offered in "Personal Meditation."

II. Personal Reflection

   A. Create spiritual/mental/physical inventory.

      1. Break up into small groups and create a profile of a "typical Christian."
         a. What kind of relationship does that person have with God?
         b. What type of self-image does that person have?
         c. How does this individual act out relationships and feelings?
         d. Is God first in this person's life? How do you know? Why or why not?

      2. In silence, ask the group members to examine *themselves,* using questions *a, b, c,* and *d.* After several minutes, quietly remind the group that doubt and fear may be our greatest obstacles to spiritual growth. Do we *really* believe in God? Does the *visible* conduct of our lives say yes or no?

   B. Discuss what others say and do.

      1. Ask several members of the group to choose one of the personal experiences from Part 2 of this book. As they are read, try to visualize that person. How does that person trust, feel, and act as a child of God?

      2. Discuss *why* persons tithe. What are the dangers of tithing? What are the benefits?

III. Old Testament Background

A. Read aloud the "Introduction" in Part 1.

B. In small groups, read and discuss the following scripture passages:

1. Genesis 28:10-22
2. Leviticus 27:30-33
3. Deuteronomy 14:22-29
4. Malachi 3:6-12

C. As a total group, consider this: If you had lived your life during the past twenty-four hours with advice from these passages, what would you have done differently?

IV. Experiences

A. Each of us is answering, moment by moment, three questions: *Who* am I? *Whose* am I? *What* on earth am I doing here? In pairs, allow time for the participants to talk about themselves:

1. Recall your parents' attitudes about money and tithing.
2. How do you feel about the tithe?
3. Are there any stumbling blocks to growing as a joyful, generous giver?
4. Is my giving a response to God, or am I playing a numbers game?

B. Ask the group members to write their own witness or experience related to tithing as a part of their commitment to God, to their personal growth, and to this study series.

V. Going Out

A. What are the challenges and opportunities each of us has while we are together and after the study sessions are completed?

1. Encourage the group members to spend time each day studying the scriptures and reflecting on their responses to God.
2. Commit to one another to be present for the three remaining sessions.
3. Reflect on the statement that tithing is not fund-raising. Tithing is a remedy for a spiritual disease that affects our relationship to God. It is a *gift* to help us put God first in our lives!

B. Close with a prayer that each will be made aware that we are being renewed and transformed. Thank God that we are becoming more honest with God, ourselves, and other people—that we are *learning* who we are, *believing* that we are created in God's image, and *acting* out our knowledge and faith.

Session Two: Attitudes and Accountability

(Suggested Time: One Hour)

I. Coming Together

A. Remind the group that spiritual discipline and growth must take place *within* Christian community; we *need* each other for personal and corporate faith development.

B. Join together in prayer for each person present, for silences when we can listen to God, for joyous celebrations when we can lift up God's miracles among us, and for tithing which helps us examine our attitudes and accountability.

C. Take time for persons to share their written reflections on tithing. (See IV. B., Session I.)

II. Personal Reflection

A. In pairs, discuss these feelings about money:
   1. When I realize I have lost money, I feel ...
   2. Being generous feels...
   3. Giving money away feels...
   4. Being broke feels...
   5. Paying bills feels...
   6. God's generosity makes me feel...

B. Remind the group that Jesus teaches us that a person's sense of well-being does not *increase* with material possessions and comforts. Our feelings and attitudes about money often get between us and God, between us and others.
   1. How does giving help or hurt relationships within a family, with others, with God?
   2. How do we live out the fact that God calls us to take responsibility for 100 percent of what we possess?

C. Again, in pairs, conduct a personal "interview" with one another

to begin to determine personal priorities in terms of faith, possessions, and personal relationships. Consider topics such as:

1. Describe the way you spend your time.
2. Share how you determine your level of giving through the
   church.
3. Determine if each person has a particular motivation for a
   closer relationship with God, a goal for increased giving.
4. Try to find out what struggles each person has in determining
   priorities.

III. What does the New Testament say?

   A. Read aloud the first paragraph of "The New Testament Tradi-
      tion" in Part 1, reminding the group that our *attitudes* are
      revealed in our actions.

   B. In small groups, read and discuss the following scripture passages:

      1. Matthew 25:14-30
      2. Luke 21:1-4
      3. 2 Corinthians 8:1-6
      4. 1 Corinthians 16:1-3

   C. As a total group, discuss the concept that tithing is a disciplined
      practice of giving to grow toward and move beyond.

      1. Where do I start?
      2. What is my goal? Why?
      3. Is there a strategy?
      4. When I get to 10 percent, how do I know God's next goal for
         me?
      5. Does my joy *really* increase as I become more generous?

IV. Experiences

   A. We are called to be stewards of God's love.

      1. In pairs, read and discuss Genesis 1:1 and John 3:16. What
         images of God do these passages offer?
      2. The gifts of God's love through the continuing creation,
         Jesus, and the promise of the eternal life lead us to respond
         to that love and act. Name ways we can act *now*—in our
         homes, in the community, in the church.
      3. Together, commit to *one* way to act as caretakers, stewards,
         of God's love between now and the next session. Is your

commitment a mental decision or a spiritual need to respond? Is your giving through the church a financial decision
or a spiritual adventure?

B. God wants us to reorder our lives.

1. Ask each person to read silently 2 Corinthians 9:7-10 and
Matthew 23:25-28.
2. Allow time for reflection and notetaking:
   a. Is there anything in my life that gets in the way of my
   relationships?
   b. Are my actions merely functional or a response to God?
   c. Do I need to reorder my economic life?

V. Going Out

A. Remind the group that growth requires inner and outward
change.

1. As each of us discovers our way in a personal journey of faith,
we need to dream and set goals, as well as evaluate where we
are right now.
2. The scriptures and times of silent reflection, listening to God,
alert us to strategies for living and open us to spiritual accountability.

B. Allow time for prayer when each person in the group may share,
silently or publicly, particular struggles or successes.

1. Go out with the reminder that most people *act* their way into
a new way of thinking.
2. Go out trusting that God is leading you to changing attitudes,
life beyond survival, and the experience of abundant, blessed
living.

Session Three: Do We Need a Miracle?

(Suggested Time: One Hour)

I. Coming Together

A. Begin to create an atmosphere of adventure and high hopes,
reminding the group that tithing is contagious. God continues to
work in miraculous and surprising ways. Today, when the pos-

sible will not do, we *need* a miracle! *Believing* in miracles, in God's power, we begin to see miracles everywhere.

B. *Silently* come together for prayer. Allow *more* time than you ordinarily would. At this mid-point of the series, the group is more prepared to listen to God working within and without.

C. Quietly end the time of silent listening to God's direction. Remind the participants that each one is created in the image of God, that the power of the Holy Spirit is now at work—in each individual, in the group, *and* in the larger congregation. This session will begin to focus on the possibilities for changing, life-renewing action.

II. Personal Reflection

A. As a group, share and record what you feel and believe the job of churches to be.

B. After you have listed the beliefs and feelings of the group, you may need to add:

1. To lead others to God through Jesus Christ.

2. To teach people, to give them the "tools" to put God first in their lives. The *tithe*, in light of the Calvary event, is one of those tools!

C. In small groups, begin to describe *who* you are as a congregation. What is happening *now*? Are you the image of God in the world?

1. *Imagine* that 50 percent of the congregation tithed. What would the yearly income be, approximately? (You may need to do some research *before* the session to approximate the present income.)

2. What ministries could you be doing that you are not presently doing?
   a. In the local congregation?
   b. In the community?
   c. In the world?

D. Come together as a group and share some of the possibilities of being a tithing church.

III. How does our heritage help or hinder us?

    A. Ask someone to read aloud "The Church Tradition" from Part I.

        1. For a few moments, quietly reflect on how the scriptures and tradition have led to the action or non-action of this time.

        2. Briefly discuss what you perceive as the chief motivations for giving today.

        3. List any excuses, rationalizations, or stumbling blocks that prevent persons from having an intimate relationship with God and a joyous, generous response to God.

    B. In pairs, share how you feel about this promise made by members of Church of the Savior, Washington, DC: "We covenant with Christ and one another to give proportionately *beginning* with a tithe of our income."

        1. Pursue the discussion by outlining a financial plan using the tithe as a *given* factor in that plan.

        2. Would that factor change for a personal financial plan? A congregational financial plan?

        3. Close the discussion with a reminder for personal meditation. A Christian decision is a decision made in freedom!

IV. Experiences

    A. Individually, begin to list some of the gifts you realize that you have to share with others.

        1. Name the specific ways you are blessed by God's abundant love (health, food, shelter, time, a loving community, God's Word revealed in the scriptures, etc.).

        2. In another column, identify those for which you are particularly grateful. How do you *claim* those gifts, "unwrap" them?

        3. Identify at least two gifts you believe you are being led to *act* on. What actions are they? What messages do they give to others?

    B. Come together as a group and list some of the gifts of the group that can be shared.

        1. Name the specific ways you feel you are being blessed be-

cause of the opportunity to explore the tithe as a way to put God first in your lives.

2. Begin to prioritize the gifts you believe you are ready to claim.

3. As a group, covenant with one another to make visible at least one action that is a direct result of your involvement with the group study. Be prepared to share and reevaluate that action at the next session.

V. Going Out

A. Share with the group this statement by a long-term tither (thirty-two years): "There are no former tithers. The very act of tithing seems to declare freedom—an experience of joy and an acceptance of God's love."

B. Ask each person to read again 2 Corinthians 8 and 9 before the next session.

C. Join hands and prepare to go out as you came together, silently, in prayer.

Session Four: Courage and Commitment

(Suggested Time: One Hour)

I. Coming Together

A. Begin the session by quoting from Frederick Buechner's *A Room Called Remember:*

Words are dangerous because for better or worse they are so powerful, and yet at the same time dangerous because they are so weak. They are weak in the sense that for all their power, they can never say all there is to say about anything, and the danger is that we are perpetually inclined to forget that.

B. Say the following before the opening prayer: "Let the words of my mouth and the meditations of my heart be acceptable in your sight, O Lord, my strength and my redeemer."

C. Pray that each person will be aware of the power of words and actions, but also aware of personal weakness. None of us can do it all. With God's help, but putting God first in our lives, we *begin* the journey and have the power to invite others to share in it.

II. Personal Reflection

    A. Look back at Session III and review the list of gifts you believe you have as a group or as a congregation.

        1. What covenant did you make with one another to act out? How did you visualize one of those gifts?

        2. Encourage group members to relate their personal experiences and feelings as they acted on that promise.

    B. In small groups, discuss briefly some of the changes (spiritual, mental, physical) that are taking place in your lives.

        1. Remember that we don't have to wait until we are perfect to do what God wants us to do!

        2. Most people adopt disciplines that allow them to remain pretty much as they are!

        3. What do you feel God expects of you? What do you expect from God?

III. What does Paul say?

    A. Most church members do about as much as they are taught.

        1. Discuss, as a group, some of the lessons Paul taught the church at Corinth.

        2. Reflect *specifically* on what Paul teaches about giving as a response to God.

    B. Describe yourselves, your group, your church. What do you imagine that Paul would want to teach you?

IV. Experiences

    A. We *must* witness. We are called to be good stewards of our own story of our relationship with God through Christ.

        1. Ask the group members to reflect on the witness or testimony that they wrote after Session I.

        2. Remind them that sharing the faith is *not* a program. *Tithing* is not a program, but a gesture of faith, of putting God first.

        3. Review some motivations for passing on the story.

            a. Each faith story is grounded in God's love.

            b. Telling the story fulfills Christ's commission to us to "Go then, to all peoples everywhere ... "

            c. Our stories *together* focus on total redemption. God's intent for all creation is not fulfilled until *all* are invited and present.

B. Ask each person to make notes for a second story of witness and experience with tithing based on participation in these sessions and personal meditation.

1. Each testimony is a personal response to God in a growing relationship with God.
2. When we respond to God and the image of God in us, we *must* share.

C. As a group, discuss times and places when these stories can be shared.

D. Begin to develop a strategy for becoming a tithing church. Here are some suggestions.

1. The pastor will commit to practice, teach, and preach tithing.
2. Tithing will be discussed and encouraged at all meetings where Christian stewardship is discussed.
3. The church will create its own dream and implement an intentional, specific program to make it come true, realizing that
   a. The Old Testament reminds us that the tithe is God's directive to the people.
   b. The tithe is a rich *blessing*.
   c. Each of us must open our ears and listen to the *personal* message of God's Word.
   d. God does not require less of New Testament Christians than God did of the children of Israel.
   e. Our tithes and gifts are symbols of response to God, acknowledging Christ's leadership, and are a specific means of growing in grace—going beyond *hearing* the gospel to *practicing* it.

4. Plan *now* for another small group adventure with *Putting God First: The Tithe*.
   a. Each participant will commit to recruit one person for the next group.
   b. Each participant will commit to continue the daily spiritual discipline of prayer, scripture reading, and meditation and will encourage one other person to do so.

V. Going Out

   A. Ask someone to read Day Fourteen in Part 3, "Personal Medita-
      tion." Include the reading of John 3:16-18.

   B. Read together "A Prayer of Response" by Ray E. Van Alstine.

   C. Spend a few moments in silence reflecting on and giving thanks
      for the opportunity for spiritual transformation.

   D. Go out as well-loved children of God, remembering your shared
      commitment.

                                                                    Shalom

A Prayer of Thanksgiving and Blessing

Thank you, God, for the task and opportunity—*whatever* the task and *whenever* the opportunity. Thank you for your love, for the love of other people, and for the tithe as a tool to help your children grow in intimate relationship with you.

Bless and keep all of those who helped this book move from idea to reality.

GLEN H. HAWORTH
GRADY O. FLOYD
LeROY E. GOSSET
W.W. DUNLAP
LLOYD S. SAATJIAN
KENNETH G. ENGLAR
CALVIN E. BREAM
PERCIVAL GRUMBEIN, JR.
JACK M. TUELL
LEON T. McKENZIE
WARREN BARCALOW
CHARLES S. BENNER
GERALD N. HANNA
J. WHEELER
REV. DAN R. KENNEDY
R. HORTON
BRUCE CONCHING
CLARENCE W. MAUERHAN
HOWARD B. DAFFRON
FRANCIS E. FEHLMAN
GERALD L. GOVAN
RAY E. VAN ALSTINE
LaVERNE E. STEVENS
MILDRED HILTS
CLEMENT G. SAMPSON
G. TOM CARTER
THE REV. EVA K. BROWN
RUTH BLAIR

DONALD H. BARNETT
  ENTERPRISES
CALIF-PACIFIC ANNUAL CONF,
  UMC
THE MULLEN TRUST—KENNETH
  I. MULLEN
JAMES K. HEMPSTEAD
SAM GOLDEN
JACKSON MILLER
ROY STEPHENSON
CHARLES WELLS
TERRY W. ALLEN
CLARA BASS
DAVIS THOMPSON
GEORGE ENGELHARDT
SANDY EDDY
THE REV. LANE BAILEY
MARIE VINSONHALER
JOAN GELHAUS
THE REV. MATTHEW GATES
ROBERT SMYTHE
MARGOT BALL
PAUL RABY
MARY BOYD
GWENDOLYN J. MYERS
JIM NORRIS
PAT STROMAN
CHEOL HWAN KWAK

Amen.

NORMA WIMBERLY GASKILL

As You Continue to Learn and Grow

The Holy Use of Money, John C. Haughey, S. J. Garden City, New York: Doubleday and Company, Inc., 1986.

Freedom of Simplicity, Richard J. Foster. San Francisco: Harper and Row, Publishers, 1981.

What Does the Lord Require?, Bruce C. Birch. Philadelphia: The Westminster Press, 1985.

The Tithe: Challenge or Legalism?, Douglas W. Johnson. Nashville: Abingdon Press, 1984.

Tzedakah, Jacob Neusner. Rossel Books, 44 Dunbar Drive, Choppaqua, New York, 1982.

Imaging God: Dominion as Stewardship, Douglas John Hall. New York: Friendship Press, 1987.

How to Develop a Tithing Church, Charlie W. Shedd. Nashville: Thomas Nelson, 1978.

Because God Gives. Nashville: Available only thru Stewardship Unit, 1986. 615-340-7075.

Now, Concerning the Offering, Hilbert J. Berger. Nashville: Discipleship Resources, 1987.

Faith-Sharing: Dynamic Christian Witnessing by Invitation, H. Eddie Fox and George E. Morris. Nashville: Discipleship Resources, 1986.

Common Thieves, Wyatt Lee Walker. New York: Martin Luther King Fellows Press, 1986.

Tithing: Gimmick or Gift? Norma Wimberly. Nashville: Discipleship Resources, 1992.

Be a Proportionate Giver, Norma Wimberly. Nashville: Discipleship Resources, 1992.

Right On The Money, Brian Bauknight. Available only through Stewardship Unit. Phone (615) 340-7075.

Christians and Money, Donald W. Joiner. Available only through Stewardship Unit. Phone (615) 340-7075.